WRITTEN ENGLISH

ROBERT RAINSBURY
The American Language Institute
New York University

WRITTEN ENGLISH

An Introduction
for Beginning Students
of English as a Second Language

PRENTICE-HALL, INC., Englewood Cliffs, New Jersey 07632

Library of Congress Cataloging in Publication Data
Rainsbury, Robert, 1925-
    Written English.

        1. English language—Text books for foreigners.
I. Title.
PE1128.R26   428.2'4   76-50132
ISBN 0-13-970673-9

Printed in the United States of America

10   9

PRENTICE-HALL INTERNATIONAL, INC., *London*
PRENTICE-HALL OF AUSTRALIA PTY. LIMITED, *Sydney*
PRENTICE-HALL OF CANADA, LTD., *Toronto*
PRENTICE-HALL OF INDIA PRIVATE LIMITED, *New Delhi*
PRENTICE-HALL OF JAPAN, INC., *Tokyo*
PRENTICE-HALL OF SOUTHEAST ASIA PTE. LTD., *Singapore*
WHITEHALL BOOKS LIMITED, *Wellington, New Zealand*

Contents

Introduction

The lessons that make up this book were created to give the beginning student of English as a foreign language intensive practice with the written language. Until recently, texts created for this field have concentrated on the development of oral skills; students seeking help in learning to write, particularly beginning students, have often been left to fend for themselves. The texts that do exist tend to concentrate on matters of style. This book, however, is intended to provide help in mastering mechanical skills. These skills include spelling and punctuation in the initial stages and sentence combining and clause making in the latter stages.

Note that these lessons were written to be used as a *supplemental* text by students who are also receiving instruction in the grammar and lexicon from some other source. For this reason, not every grammar term used is explained and not every principle is illustrated. In Lesson Seven, for example, the student is required in some sentences to make a change from *a* to *an*. The rule for this is not given. It is assumed that by the time the student reaches this point in any grammar course, he will have been taught this rule. The exercise is used to drill rather than to introduce the rule.

Reintroduction of previously learned material is one of the principal strategies employed in the lessons. In Lesson One, for example, the student's attention is directed to matters of punctuation. In addition, however, the unpunctuated sentences force the student to distinguish between statement and question, thus drilling the word order. Teachers should be alert for other drills that present similar challenges. Thus, in Lesson Two, in a drill on short answers, the student must decide where one sentence ends and another begins. In Lesson Three, the student must remember the previously introduced rule about capitalization of place names. Two things, then, should be remembered by the teacher who presents these lessons. First, there is a carefully worked out continuity from one exercise to the next, from one lesson to the next. Second, there is an unstressed component in almost every lesson which is as important as that which is stressed.

How to Use This Book

The material in this workbook is designed to be used during the class period. Each lesson is designed to cover approximately one class hour. The following procedure for presenting the lesson is suggested:

1. The teacher explains the rule the text and examples set forth. Little attempt has been made to simplify the language of the explanations. Therefore, the teacher must, through the use of blackboard examples or any other method (including Cuisenaire rods!), show the students what is involved.

2. When the teacher is sure that the explanation has been understood, the exercises should be done immediately. The teacher can then move about the room checking and answering questions as the students work.

3. When all the explanations have been completed and all the exercises written, the model paragraph will have been reached. For the first twelve lessons, the teacher can simply read the paragraph with the students, making sure that every student understands it.

4. The students should then do the final exercise. Students should benefit more by not being able to use the model as a crutch. The exercise thus becomes a real test of acquired skill and not merely a copying exercise. In Lessons Eight and Ten, however, the final exercise differs slightly from the others in this first section. Here, the student has a partially completed paragraph for which he or she must supply the missing element. In Lesson Eight, this is an easy task—the student simply supplies the names of persons he or she knows. In Lesson Ten, however, although the missing words are also supplied from the student student's own experience, he or she is forced, in addition, to distinguish between uncountable nouns and singular and plural countable nouns.

5. The final lessons, 13 through 19, are in four parts rather than two. It is expected that they will be taught in *two* segments, one hour for Parts I and II, one hour for Parts III and IV. The first two parts follow the format of the first twelve lessons. Part III of each of these final lessons reviews the material of the first two parts briefly, and then Part IV provides a topic for free composition. The students should be given all the remaining time after the completion of Part III to write the composition. Before they begin, however, the teacher should remind them of the grammatical focus of the lesson and see that they practice it in the composition. This is particularly true of Lessons Fifteen and Sixteen. In each of these lessons, a list of verbs is provided and the student is asked to use as many of them as possible, but a minimum of five, in the composition. The teacher should stress these instructions, since if the students do not practice the regular verbs in Lesson Fifteen and the irregular verbs in Lesson Sixteen, the point of the lesson is lost. As has been noted, not every grammar term used in the lesson is explained. If the student is receiving simultaneous instruction in grammar, this should pose no problem, but the teacher should always make sure that the student understands the task he or she is performing and the reason for it.

It is my hope that this book will enable the beginning student to practice the sometimes complex, subtle, and vexing problems which written English poses. I hope, at the same time, that the teacher will find it a stimulating experience to guide the student through these lessons. Their preparation and teaching have certainly been an exciting adventure for me. I am indebted to many for making this adventure possible, but I would especially like to thank the director of the American Language Institute, Milton Saltzer, for giving me the opportunity to prepare these lessons. I would also like to thank my colleagues, Miriam Dancy and Marcia Cohen, for their valuable and often stringent criticism. Finally, I owe a particular debt of gratitude to Jean Praninskas for her careful reading of the original manuscript and her many suggestions and criticisms; they contributed greatly to the final form of the book.

ABCDEFGHIJKLMNOPQRSTUVWXYZ
abcdefghijklmnopqrstuvwxyz

WRITTEN ENGLISH

LESSON 1
Punctuation

PART I
Sentences (initial capital, end punctuation); Apostrophe with Verb Contractions

SENTENCES

Statements begin with a capital letter and end with a period.

EXAMPLE   <u>T</u>he boy is happy<u>.</u>

EXERCISE   *In the spaces provided below the sentences, copy each sentence, adding capital letters and periods.*

1. the girl is pretty

2. the actor is handsome

3. the men are teachers

4. the woman is a doctor

5. the women are tall

Questions begin with a capital letter and end with a question mark.

EXAMPLE   <u>I</u>s the boy happy<u>?</u>

EXERCISE   *In the spaces provided, copy each sentence, adding capital letters and question marks.*

1. is the man tall

2. is the man a lawyer

3. are the women lawyers

4. is the woman short

5. are the men teachers

In the spaces provided, copy each sentence, adding capital letters and periods or question marks.

    1. the girl is young

    2. are the men lawyers

    3. is the boy fat

    4. the men are nurses

    5. the women are actresses

    6. is the woman a teacher

THE APOSTROPHE WITH VERB CONTRACTIONS

In a verb contraction in a statement, the apostrophe replaces the letter that is not in the word.

EXAMPLE   The <u>boy is</u> a student.
              The <u>boy's</u> a student.

EXERCISE   *Copy each sentence, adding capital letters, periods, and apostrophes.*

    1. the boys happy

    2. the girls pretty

    3. the mans a nurse

    4. the womans tall

    5. the childs fat

    6. the womans an engineer

The apostrophe is also used in negative verb contractions.

EXAMPLE   The man <u>isn't</u> a teacher.
              The women <u>aren't</u> nurses.

EXERCISE   *In the spaces provided, copy each sentence, adding capital letters, periods, and apostrophes.*

    1. the boy isnt sad

    2. the women arent secretaries

    3. the girl isnt a student

    4. the men arent doctors

5. the woman isnt a nurse

6. the girls arent tall

The apostrophe is *not* used with nouns in plural statements because no contraction is made. (There is one exception to this rule. We will learn it later.)

EXAMPLE   The boys are students.

EXERCISE   *In the spaces provided, copy each sentence, adding capital letters, periods, and apostrophes, if they are necessary.*

1. the boys a student

2. the boys are students

3. the girls pretty

4. the girls are pretty

5. the doctors tall

6. the doctors are tall

The apostrophe is used in verb contractions in statements with pronouns. In this case, plurals may be contracted.

EXAMPLE   The boy is happy.
           The boy's happy.
           He is happy.
           He's happy.
           The boys are happy.
           They are happy.
           They're happy.

EXERCISE   *In the spaces provided, copy each sentence, adding capital letters, periods, and apostrophes.*

1. hes sad

2. shes a secretary

3. theyre doctors

4. were students

5. youre a teacher

6. im a lawyer

In negative contractions with pronouns, two forms are used.

EXAMPLE   He <u>is not</u> happy.
He <u>isn't</u> happy.
<u>He's not</u> happy.
They <u>are not</u> happy.
They <u>aren't</u> happy.
<u>They're not</u> happy.

EXERCISE   *In the spaces provided, copy each sentence adding capital letters, periods, and apostrophes.*

    1. he isnt fat

    2. shes not a nurse

    3. they arent secretaries

    4. im a doctor

    5. you arent lawyers

PART II
Model Paragraph

Read and study this paragraph carefully.

      The woman's a secretary. She's pretty. She's intelligent. She's happy. She's not sad.

      The girls are students. They're pretty. They're intelligent. They're happy. They aren't sad.

EXERCISE   *Cover the Model Paragraph with a piece of paper. Copy the sentences below, in paragraph form as they are on the page. Add all necessary punctuation.*

      the womans a secretary shes pretty shes intelligent shes happy shes not sad

      the women are secretaries theyre pretty theyre intelligent theyre happy they arent sad

LESSON 2
Capitalization and Punctuation

PROPER NOUNS

Names of persons begin with capital letters.

EXAMPLES   Bob Jones
Susan Baker

Titles used with names begin with capital letters also.

EXAMPLE   Mr. Brown (notice the period)
President Jones
Miss Susan Baker
Ms. Sharon White (notice the period)
Mrs. Waters (notice the period)
Dr. Johnson (notice the period)

If a word is *not* used as a title, it does not begin with a capital letter.

EXAMPLE   Jonas Salk is a doctor.
Alvin Jones is the president.

EXERCISE   *In the space provided, copy each sentence, adding all necessary punctuation.*

1. bob and tom are students

2. mrs jones is a homemaker

3. mr thomas is a teacher

4. mr ward is a lawyer

5. miss walker is a nurse

6. dr williams is a poet

7. alberts a pianist

8. johns a teacher

Names of *countries, nationalities,* and *languages* begin with capital letters.

EXAMPLE   Mr. Gomez is from Venezuela.
Mr. Dubois is French.
Anna's language is Spanish.
Carlos is Colombian.

EXERCISE   *Copy each sentence, adding all necessary punctuation.*

1. is maria from ecuador

2. mrs braun is german

3. are the women from peru

4. is mrs walewskas language polish or russian

5. dr guardino is italian

THE COMMA

In a short answer, *yes* and *no* are separated from the rest of the sentence by a comma.

EXAMPLE   Yes, he is.
No, they aren't.

EXERCISE   *Copy each sentence, adding all necessary punctuation.*

1. is bob a doctor   yes he is

2. are the women waitresses yes they are

3. is dr johnson a frenchman no he isnt

4. is mary tired   yes she is

5. is this a grammar book   no it isnt

Items in a series are separated by commas. It is necessary to use a comma before *and* and *or*.

EXAMPLE   Mary, Helen, Betty, and Grace are nurses.

EXERCISE   *In the space provided, copy each sentence, putting in all necessary punctuation.*

1. bob tom and george are students

6

2. colombia ecuador brazil and peru are in south america

3. the three languages of switzerland are french german and italian

4. helga ernst maren and josef are german

THE PERIOD

A short answer is a complete sentence. Anything that comes after is a new sentence and begins with a capital letter.

EXAMPLE   Yes, he is. <u>He</u>'s a doctor.

EXERCISE   *Copy each sentence, adding all necessary punctuation.*

1. are the children tired   yes they are theyre tired

2. is the woman intelligent   yes she is shes intelligent

3. are the workers busy   yes they are theyre busy

4. is the woman a good lawyer   yes she is shes a good lawyer

5. are the men doctors   yes they are theyre doctors

PRONOUNS

When we write two sentences together with the same subject, we can use a pronoun for the subject of the second sentence.

EXAMPLE   The boy is a student.   <u>He</u> is intelligent.
               The women are nurses.   <u>They</u> are skillful.

Note: The pronoun <u>I</u> is *always* written with a capital letter.

EXERCISE   *In the space provided, copy each sentence. In the second sentence, put a pronoun in place of the underlined words. Add all necessary punctuation.*

1. miss brown is a student   <u>miss brown</u> is pretty

2. the boys sick   <u>the boys</u> in bed

3. my brother is a businessman   <u>my brother</u> is rich

4. the girls are teachers   <u>the girls</u> are busy

5. mary and i are students   <u>mary and i</u> are working

Read the following paragraph and study it carefully.

The Students in the Class

Maria Gomez is in the first row. She is Venezuelan. Karl Freund is in the second row. He is behind Miss Gomez. He is from Germany. Pierre Dubois, Joseph Lagrange, and Joseph Lacroix are in the third row. They are Haitian. Dr. Chen is in the last row. He is Chinese. He is from Taiwan.

EXERCISE   *Cover the Model Paragraph with a piece of paper. Copy the following paragraph, putting a pronoun in place of each underlined group of words. Add all necessary punctuation.*

maria gomez is in the first row maria gomez is venezuelan karl freund is in the second row karl freund is behind miss gomez karl freund is from germany pierre dubois, joseph lagrange and joseph lacroix are in the third row pierre dubois joseph lagrange and joseph lacroix are haitian dr chen is in the last row dr chen is a medical doctor dr chen is chinese dr chen is from taiwan

LESSON 3
Possessive Pronouns

PART I
The Apostrophe with Possessives

THE APOSTROPHE

The apostrophe is used with a proper noun to show possession. It is *never* used with a possessive pronoun.

EXAMPLE   Is this book <u>Tom's?</u>   No, it's <u>yours</u>

Note: <u>It's</u> (with an apostrophe) is the contracted form of <u>it is.</u> <u>Its</u> (without an apostrophe) is the possessive form of the pronoun <u>it</u>.

EXERCISE   *In the space provided, copy each sentence, putting in apostrophes and all other necessary punctuation.*

1. is this book yours   no its johns

2. are these books toms   no theyre hers

3. is that car theirs   no its mr browns

4. is this pen hers   no its marys

POSSESSIVE PRONOUNS AND ADJECTIVES

A noun following a possessive can be taken out of a sentence if it has been previously mentioned or if the meaning is clear to the reader.

EXAMPLE   My tie is red.   <u>John's</u> tie is blue.
                My tie is red.   <u>John's</u> is blue.
                Is that your car?   No, it's <u>John's</u> car.
                Is that your car?   No, it's <u>John's</u>.

EXERCISE   *In the space provided, copy the sentences. Take the <u>underlined</u> word out of the second sentence in each group. Put in all necessary punctuation.*

1. is this bills hat   no its toms <u>hat</u>

2. are these your books   no theyre joes <u>books</u>

3. is this your newspaper   no its bills <u>newspaper</u>

4. are these joes books   no theyre sams <u>books</u>

5. is this your office   no its freds <u>office</u>

---

1. my hat is big   johns <u>hat</u> is small

2. my apartment is small   maries <u>apartment</u> is big

3. my car is new   joes <u>car</u> is old

4. bills sister is fat   georges <u>sister</u> is thin

5. johns book is interesting   toms <u>book</u> is boring

---

1. my office is on main st   johns <u>office</u> is on state st

2. my house is on broad st   bills <u>house</u> is on green st

3. my apartment is on the fifth floor   tims <u>apartment</u> is on the tenth floor

4. my wife is a secretary   harrys <u>wife</u> is a nurse

5. my camera is new   franks <u>camera</u> is old

A possessive pronoun can take the place of a possessive *and* the following noun.

EXAMPLE   John's tie is red.   <u>My tie</u> is blue.
                John's tie is red.   <u>Mine</u> is blue.

EXERCISE   *In the space provided, copy each sentence. Put possessive pronouns in place of the <u>underlined</u> words. Add all necessary punctuation.*

1. is that his book   no its <u>her book</u>

2. is that her chair   no its <u>his chair</u>

3. is that your car   no its <u>his car</u>

4. is this my notebook   no its <u>her notebook</u>

5. are these our seats   no theyre <u>their seats</u>

6. is this his homework   no its <u>our homework</u>

---

1. my car is old   <u>his car</u> is new

2. their books are heavy   <u>our books</u> are light

3. her father is a doctor   <u>his father</u> is a lawyer

4. our teacher is a man   <u>their teacher</u> is a woman

5. my apartment is big   <u>her apartment</u> is small

6. my tie is red   <u>your tie</u> is green

---

1. is this your book   no it isnt <u>my book</u> is red

2. is this my car   no it isnt <u>your car</u> is new

3. are these her shoes   no they arent <u>her shoes</u> are brown

4. are those his brothers   no they arent <u>his brothers</u> are tall

5. is that our teacher   no it isnt <u>our teacher</u> is young

6. is this their house   no it isnt <u>their house</u> is on the corner

PART II
Model Paragraph

My home is on Main St. John's is on Broad St. John's apartment is small. Mine is large. My rent is high. John's is low. John's salary is large. Mine is small. My family is large. John's is small. John's problems are few. Mine are many.

Copy the following paragraph. Add all necessary punctuation.
Take out <u>underlined</u> *words and put possessive pronouns*
where they are needed.

    my house is on main st johns <u>house</u> is on broad st johns apartment
is small <u>my apartment</u> is large my rent is high johns <u>rent</u> is low johns
salary is large <u>my salary</u> is small my family is large johns <u>family</u> is
small johns problems are few <u>my problems</u> are many

LESSON 4
Noun Plurals

PART I
Plurals with -s, -es, -ves, -ies

We form the plural of nouns by adding -s

EXAMPLE   There is a book on the desk.
There are two <u>books</u> on the desk.

EXERCISE   *In the space provided, copy each sentence, changing the word in parentheses to the plural form. Add all necessary punctuation.*

1. there are two (pen) on the table

2. there are (word) on the blackboard

3. there are three (room) in johns apartment

4. his three (son) are (student)

5. there are two red (tie) in the drawer

6. there are ten (floor) in this building

7. there are two (bed) in the bedroom

8. there are six (egg) in the refrigerator

9. my two (sister) are (teacher)

10. there are many (desk) in the classroom

When a noun ends in -s, -z, -ch, -sh, -x, we form the plural by adding -es

EXAMPLE   There is a dish on the table.
There are two <u>dishes</u> on the table.

In the space provided, copy each sentence, changing the word in parentheses to the plural form. Add all necessary punctuation.

   1. there are ten (glass) in the kitchen

   2. there are some (box) on the floor

   3. there are two (sandwich) in the refrigerator

   4. there are many (class) in this building

In the space provided, copy each sentence, changing the word in parentheses to the plural form. Add all necessary punctuation.

   1. there are some (book) on the table

   2. there are two (door) in this room

   3. there are some (dress) in her closet

   4. there are some (teacher) in the hall

   5. there are some (watch) in the store window

   6. there are (cross) in the church

   7. there are some (girl) in the cafeteria

   8. there are some (brush) on the dresser

Most nouns that end in -o also form the plural with -es.

There is a tomato in the refrigerator.
There are two tomatoes in the refrigerator.

There are a few exceptions to this rule.

solo   solos
piano   pianos

In the space provided, copy each sentence, changing the word in parentheses to the plural form. Add all necessary punctuation.

   1. there are some (potato) in the refrigerator

   2. there are (piano) in the music store

   3. there are two (tomato) on the table

When a noun ends in an -e that is not pronounced, we add only -s.

EXAMPLE   There is a sentence on the blackboard.
           There are two <u>sentences</u> on the blackboard.

EXERCISE   *In the space provided, copy each sentence, changing the noun in parentheses to the plural form. Add all necessary punctuation.*

    1.   there are three (house) in the picture

    2.   there are (nurse) in the hospital

    3.   there are five (bottle) on the shelf

    4.   there are many (picture) in the book

    5.   there are four (plate) on the table.

Many words that end in -f or -fe, change the -f or -fe to -ve in the plural.

EXAMPLE   There is a knife on the table.
           There are two <u>knives</u> on the table.

Some words ending in -f do not make this change.

EXAMPLE   roof   <u>roofs</u>
           handkerchief   <u>handkerchiefs</u>

EXERCISE   *In the space provided, copy each sentence, changing the noun in parentheses to the plural form. Add all necessary puntuation.*

    1.   the (leaf) on the (tree) are green

    2.   there is snow on the (roof) of the (house)

    3.   there are two (loaf) of bread in the refrigerator

When a noun ends in -y with a *consonant* before it, we change the -y to -ie to form the plural.

EXAMPLE   There is a story in the book.
           There are many <u>stories</u> in the book.

EXERCISE   *In the space provided, copy each sentence, changing the noun in parentheses to the plural form. Add all necessary punctuation.*

    1.   there are two (secretary) in the office

    2.   there are (daisy) in the garden

    3.   there are (strawberry) in the refrigerator

When a noun ends in -y with a *vowel* before it, do not change the -y to -ie.

EXAMPLE   There is a tray on the table.
           There are two <u>trays</u> on the table.

EXERCISE   *In the space provided, copy each sentence, changing the noun in parentheses to the plural form. Add all necessary punctuation.*

    1.   there are seven (day) in a week

    2.   there are some (toy) in the babys room

    3.   there are six new (boy) in my class

EXERCISE   *In the space provided, copy each sentence, changing the noun in parentheses to the plural form. Add all necessary punctuation.*

    1.   there are three (key) in my pocket

    2.   there are five (penny) on the table

    3.   there are two (baby) in the picture

    4.   there are two new (toy) in the store

    5.   there are two young (boy) in the picture

Some plural forms are irregular and do not follow any rule.

EXAMPLE   There is a man on the corner.
           There are two <u>men</u> on the corner.
           There is a woman in the store.
           There are two <u>women</u> in the store.
           There is a child in the classroom.
           There are a lot of <u>children</u> in the classroom.
           There is a sheep in the field.
           There are a lot of <u>sheep</u> in the field.
           There is a fish in the refrigerator.
           There are many <u>fish</u> in the ocean.

EXERCISE   *In the space provided, copy each sentence, changing the noun in parentheses to the plural form. Add all necessary punctuation.*

    1.   there are three (child) in the hall

    2.   there are some young (man) from mexico in my class

    3.   there are some (sheep) from asia in the zoo

4. there are some (woman) in the office

5. there are some (fish) in the lake

EXERCISE *In the space provided, copy each sentence, changing the noun in parentheses to the plural form. Add all necessary punctuation.*

1. there are three new (baby) at the hospital

2. there are clean (handkerchief) in the drawer

3. there are three (man) in the hall

4. there are some (glass) in the kitchen

5. there are a lot of (child) in the park

6. there are two (knife) on the table

7. there are two (window) in this room

8. there are (plate) in the kitchen

9. there are (glass) on the table

10. there are thirty (day) in this month

When we show possession with plural nouns, we put an apostrophe *after* the plural -s.

EXAMPLE   the boy's books
the boys' books

With irregular plurals, we show possession in the usual way.

EXAMPLE   the child's books
the children's books

EXERCISE   *In the space provided, copy each sentence, adding all necessary punctuation.*

1. the childrens school is on broad st

2. the students cafeteria is in the basement

3. the boys father is a police officer

This is my children's room. There are books on the bed. The pages of the books are torn. There are socks on the floor. The socks are dirty. There are glasses on the bed table. The glasses are also dirty. There are pieces of bread and jars of peanut butter and jam near the glasses. There are knives in the jars. The knives are dirty, too.

EXERCISE   *Cover the Model Paragraph with a piece of paper. Copy the following paragraph, putting all the nouns in parentheses in plural form and adding all necessary punctuation.*

this is my (child) room there are (book) on the floor the (page) of the (book) are torn there are (sock) on the floor the (sock) are dirty there are (glass) on the bed table the (glass) are also dirty there are (piece) of bread and (jar) of peanut butter and jam near the (glass) there are (knife) in the (jar) the (knife) are dirty too

18

PART I
Auxiliary Verbs;
Spelling Changes

We show that something is happening at the moment of speaking by using a form of the verb be in the present as an *auxiliary* or extra verb, and adding -ing to the main verb. Several spelling rules are involved. We will study them one at a time, as in the last lesson.

EXAMPLE   The boys are studying now.
John is reading now.

When we use the singular form of the auxiliary, a contraction is possible.

EXAMPLE   John's reading now.

We do not normally use this contraction in formal writing, and we will not practice it in this lesson.

When a word ends in two consonants, we simply add -ing to the verb.

EXAMPLE   work   John is working now.

EXERCISE   *In the space provided, copy each sentence, adding the correct form of be and adding -ing to the verb in parentheses. Add all necessary punctuation.*

1. those students (learn) a new spelling rule

2. the child (rest) now

3. the artist (paint) a picture now

4. prof harrison (teach) his class now

5. mr and mrs watson (watch) television now

6. the men (wash) the dishes now

.en a verb ends in **-y,** we simply add **-ing** to the verb.

EXAMPLE   buy   The student is <u>buying</u> a book now.

EXERCISE   *In the space provided, copy each sentence, adding the correct form of be and adding -ing to the verb in parentheses. Add all necessary punctuation.*

1. the children (play) in the park

2. those students (try) to understand the lesson

3. the doctor (carry) his bag

4. the birds (fly) to a warm country

5. the sick boy (stay) home today

Words that end in an unpronounced final e drop the e before adding -ing.

EXAMPLE   smoke   John is <u>smoking</u> a cigar now.

EXERCISE   *In the space provided, copy each sentence, adding the correct form of be, dropping the final e and adding -ing to the verb in parentheses. Add all necessary punctuation.*

1. mr adams (shave) now

2. maria (practice) english now

3. the athletes (take) a shower now

4. the waitress (serve) coffee now

5. mr foster (give) an examination now

6. carlos (write) a letter in spanish now

EXERCISE   *In the space provided, copy each sentence, adding the correct form of be and the correctly spelled -ing form of the verb in parentheses.*

1. john (have) breakfast now

2. felipe (help) carlos with his homework

3. the children (laugh) at a funny story

4. the carpenter (make) a table

5. the students (take) a test now

20

6. mr jones (fish) in the river now

7. bill (shine) his shoes now

8. we (study) our lesson now

When a word ends in a single vowel and a consonant, we double the consonant before adding -ing.

EXAMPLE stop   the car is <u>stopping</u> now.

EXERCISE *In the space provided, copy each sentence, add the correct form of <u>be</u>, double the final consonant, and add <u>-ing</u> to the verb in parentheses.*

1. catherine wilson (shop) now

2. the children (run) down the street now

3. the students (sit) in their seats now

4. the waitress (cut) the cake now

5. carlos (put) the letter in the envelope now

6. the carpenter (hit) the nail with the hammer

If the final syllable of a word ending in a single vowel and a consonant is not accented, we do not double the final consonant before adding -ing.

EXAMPLE open   John is <u>opening</u> the letter now.

EXERCISE *In the space provided, copy each sentence, adding the correct form of <u>be</u> and adding <u>-ing</u> to the verb in parentheses. Do **not** double the final consonant.*

1. the students (listen) to the teacher now

2. the customer (order) coffee now

3. the child (butter) his toast now

If the verb ends in two vowels and a consonant, we do *not* double the final consonant before adding -ing.

EXAMPLE read   John is <u>reading</u> now.

EXERCISE *In the space provided, copy each sentence, adding the correct form of <u>be</u> and adding <u>-ing</u> to the verb in parentheses. Do **not** double the final consonant.*

1. the baby (sleep) now

2. the boys (eat breakfast) now

3. the teacher (speak) english now

4. the maid (clean) the room now

5. bill harris (feel) much better now

EXERCISE *In the space provided, copy each sentence, adding the correct form of be and adding -ing to the verb in parentheses. Make all necessary spelling changes.*

1. mary (eat) a sandwich now

2. taro (write) to his parents

3. the bus (stop) at the corner now

4. the cowboy (ride) his horse

5. the athlete (run) around the track

6. mrs bradford (cook) dinner now

7. pedro (dream) about his girl friend

8. the police officer (put) on his uniform

9. the bus driver (drive) the bus

10. the leaders (play) cards now

PART II
Model Paragraph

This is the cafeteria. Some students are standing in line. The attendants are serving the food. They are putting the food on the plates. Some students are paying for their lunches. The cashier is collecting money and making change. Other students are sitting at tables, eating sandwiches and drinking coffee.

EXERCISE   *Copy the following paragraph, putting all the verbs in parentheses in the -ing form. Add the correct form of be to each sentence, and make all necessary spelling changes. Add all necessary punctuation.*

this is the cafeteria some students (stand) in line the attendants (serve) the food they (put) the food on the plates some students (pay) for their lunch the cashier (collect) money and (make) change other students (sit) at tables, (eat) sandwiches and (drink) coffee

LESSON 6
Capitalization and Prepositions of Place

PART I
Proper Nouns;
Prepositions of Place

CAPITAL LETTERS

Names of states, cities, and streets are capitalized.

EXAMPLE   Los Angeles
California
Fifth Avenue
State Street

EXERCISE   *Copy each sentence, adding all necessary punctuation.*

1. is chicago in new jersey

2. the hospital is on main street

3. dallas is in texas

4. the school is on central avenue

Names of famous places such as museums, historic buildings, and landmarks begin with capital letters.

EXAMPLE   The Washington Monument is very tall.
Niagara Falls is a beautiful sight.
The Whitney Museum of American Art is in New York.

Note: **Prepositions, conjunctions, and other function words are not usually capitalized.**

EXERCISED   *In the space provided, copy each sentence, adding all necessary punctuation.*

1. buckingham palace is in london

2. the prado is a museum in spain

Name _____ Date _____   **25**

3. the hermitage is an art gallery in leningrad

4. frank is visiting the world trade center in new york

5. mary is taking a picture of the tower of london

PREPOSITIONS OF PLACE

We use *in* with large, general areas such as countries, cities, and states, and with buildings and rooms.

EXAMPLE   Milan is <u>in</u> Italy.

EXERCISE   *In the space provided, copy each sentence, putting <u>in</u> in place of the blank and adding all necessary punctuation.*

1. caracas is _____ venezuela

2. new delhi is _____ india

3. warsaw is _____ poland

4. cali is _____ colombia

5. bonn is _____ west germany

EXERCISE   *In the space provided, copy each sentence, putting <u>in</u> in place of the blank and adding all necessary punctuation.*

1. boston is _____ massachusetts

2. los angeles is _____ california

3. houston is _____ texas

4. chicago is _____ illinois

5. miami is _____ florida

EXERCISE   *In the space provided, copy each sentence, putting <u>in</u> in place of the blank and adding all necessary punctuation.*

1. our class is _____ room 55

2. room 55 is _____ the main building

3. the cafeteria is _____ the student center

4. the refrigerator is _____ the kitchen

5. the washing machine is _____ the laundry room

We also use <u>in</u> to indicate that something is *inside* something else.

EXAMPLE   The milk is <u>in</u> the glass.

EXERCISE   *In the space provided, copy each sentence, putting <u>in</u> in place of the blank and adding all necessary punctuation.*

    1. my handkerchief is _____ my pocket

    2. my ruler is _____ the desk drawer

    3. the cheese is _____ the refrigerator

    4. john is putting sugar _____ his coffee

    5. marys holding her pen _____ her hand

We use <u>on</u> with smaller, more specific areas such as streets and the floors of buildings.

EXAMPLE   The hospital is <u>on</u> 19th Street.

EXERCISE   *In the space provided, copy each sentence, putting <u>in</u> in place of the blank and adding all necessary punctuation.*

    1. the bank is _____ main street

    2. the house is _____ northern boulevard

    3. the theater is _____ jerome avenue

    4. the restaurant is _____ 8th street

    5. the department store is _____ broadway

EXAMPLE   Room 55 is <u>on</u> the fifth floor.

EXERCISE   *In the space provided, copy each sentence, putting <u>on</u> in place of the blank and adding all necessary punctuation.*

    1. the directors office is _____ the second floor

    2. there is a swimming pool _____ the roof

    3. my apartment is _____ the tenth floor

There are a few exceptions.

EXAMPLE   There is a laundry room <u>in</u> the basement.
                  There are public telephones <u>in</u> the lobby.

We also use <u>on</u> to indicate that something is *touching* something else.

In the space provided, copy the sentences, putting <u>on</u> in place of the blank and adding all necessary punctuation.

1. the book is _____ top of the desk

2. the bookcase is resting _____ the floor

3. john is putting his hat _____ his head

4. mary is lying _____ the couch

5. i put a bandage _____ my cut finger

EXERCISE *In the space provided, copy each sentence, putting <u>in</u> or <u>on</u> in the blank and adding all necessary punctuation.*

1. there are comfortable chairs _____ the student center

2. there is a clock _____ the wall

3. there are two dollar bills _____ my wallet

4. the teacher is writing the sentences _____ the blackboard

5. pierre is eating his lunch _____ the cafeteria

6. the museum of the city of new york is _____ fifth avenue

7. newark is _____ new jersey

8. carlos is putting a ring _____ marias finger

9. the dentists office is _____ the tenth floor

10. the taj mahal is _____ india

PART II
Model Paragraph

This is Mrs. Brown's refrigerator. There are many things in it. There is a carton on the top shelf with milk in it. There are some cookies in a box on the second shelf. There is some hamburger on a plate next to the cookies. There are some tomatoes in a paper bag on the bottom shelf. There is a large carton with ice cream in it in the freezer.

Copy the following paragraph, putting <u>on</u> or <u>in</u> in place of the blanks and adding all necessary punctuation.

this is mrs browns refrigerator there are many things _____ it

there is a carton _____ the top shelf with milk _____ it

there are some cookies _____ a box _____ the second shelf

there is some hamburger _____ a plate next to the cookies there are

some tomatoes _____ a paper bag _____ the bottom shelf there

is a large carton with ice cream _____ it _____ the freezer

LESSON 7
Combining Sentences I

Making Two Sentences into One

METHOD 1

EXAMPLE   The boy is tall.   The boy is handsome.   <u>The boy is tall and handsome.</u>
The musician is singing.   The musician is playing the piano
<u>The musician is singing and playing the piano.</u>

EXERCISE   *In the space provided, combine each pair of sentences into one using method 1:*

1. the apples are red   the apples are ripe

2. the men are skillful   the men are intelligent

3. the children are happy   the children are well

4. the teacher is tall   the teacher is strong

5. the coffee is strong   the coffee is hot

---

1. the students are writing   the students are thinking

2. the actors are singing   the actors are dancing

3. the man is talking   the man is laughing

4. the women are studying   the women are working

5. the teacher is speaking   the teacher is writing on the blackboard

METHOD 2

EXAMPLE   The boy is young.   The boy is a student.   <u>The boy is a young student.</u>
(Note the position of the article)

The boys are young.   The boys are students.   <u>The boys are young students.</u>
(See Lesson 9 and 10).

EXERCISE   *In the space provided, combine each pair of sentences into one sentence by using method 2. Add all necessary punctuation.*

1. the girl is tall   the girl is a student

2. the man is clever   the man is a lawyer

3. the women are skillful   the women are doctors

4. the girls are good   the girls are secretaries

5. the artist is talented   the artist is a painter

6. the women are beautiful   the women are actresses

7. paul newman is handsome   paul newman is a movie star

8. jonas salk is famous   jonas salk is a doctor

PART II
Model Paragraph

Our classroom is large and comfortable. It is a cheerful room. The chairs are large and wide. They are comfortable chairs. The lights are big and bright. They are excellent lights. The windows are wide and clean. Our classroom is a happy place.

EXERCISE   *Copy the following sentences, combining each pair of underlined sentences, using method 1 or method 2 as indicated. Add all necessary punctuation.*

our classroom is large our classroom is comfortable (method 1) it is cheerful it is a room (method 2) the chairs are large the chairs are wide (method 1) they are comfortable they are chairs (method 2) the lights are big the lights are bright (method 1) they are excellent they are lights (method 2) the windows are wide the windows are clean (method 1) our classroom is happy our clasroom is a place (method 2)

33

PART III
Another Method
of Combining Two Sentences into One

METHOD 3

EXAMPLE   John is a student.   Tom is a student.   <u>John and Tom are students.</u>

EXERCISE   *In the space provided, combine each pair of sentences into one sentence using method 3. Add all necessary punctuation.*

1. mary is a secretary   alice is a secretary

2. paul is a doctor   philip is a doctor

3. charles dickens is a famous writer   victor hugo is a famous writer

4. san francisco is a beautiful city   paris is a beautiful city

5. georgia is a southern state   florida is a southern state

6. the mona lisa is a famous painting   the last supper is a famous painting

7. joe is a rich lawyer   harry is a rich lawyer

PART IV
Model Paragraph

The Students in the Class

Joao and Carmen are Brazilians. Erika and Helga are medical students from Germany. Michael and Dimitrios are lawyers from Greece. Pierre and Klaus are Swiss bankers.

Copy the paragraph below and combine each pair of
underlined sentences into one sentence, using method 3.
Add all necessary punctuation.

joao is a brazilian carmen is a brazilian erika is a medical student
from germany helga is a medical student from germany michael is a
lawyer from greece dimitrios is a lawyer from greece pierre is a swiss
banker klaus is a swiss banker.

LESSON 8
Combining Sentences II

METHOD 4

EXAMPLE   John is studying chemistry.   Fred is studying chemistry.
<u>John is studying chemistry and Bill is too.</u>

EXERCISE   *In the space provided, combine each pair of sentences into*
one sentence, using method 4. Add all necessary punctuation.

1. dr wilson is a dentist   dr ross is a dentist

2. the teacher is speaking english   the students are speaking english

3. jorge is from peru   luis is from peru

4. the girls are smiling   the boys are smiling

5. tom is tired   bill is tired

6. these men are lawyers   those men are lawyers

7. ivan is a russian   katya is a russian

8. im wearing a blue shirt   harrys wearing a blue shirt

METHOD 5

We can also combine two *negative* sentences.

EXAMPLE   The teacher isn't speaking Spanish.   The students aren't speaking Spanish.
<u>The teacher isn't speaking Spanish and the student's aren't either.</u>

Notice that with negative sentences we use the word <u>either.</u>

In the space provided, combine each pair of sentences into one sentence, using method 5. Add all necessary punctuation.

1. mary isnt well   louise isnt well

2. the boys arent resting   the girls arent resting

3. alicia isnt from colombia   maria isnt from colombia

4. this room isnt a classroom   that room isnt a classroom

5. the coffee isnt hot   the food isnt hot

6. mr fielding isnt working today   his employees arent working today

7. the books arent expensive   the writing paper isnt expensive

EXERCISE *In the space provided, combine each pair of sentences into one sentence using method 4 or 5. Add all necessary punctuation.*

1. the chairs are comfortable   the sofa is comfortable

2. the doorbell isnt ringing   the telephone isnt ringing

3. the steak is delicious   the potatoes are delicious

4. the chalk is on the shelf   the eraser is on the shelf

5. dr fields isnt here   dr foster isnt here

6. monday isnt a holiday   tuesday isnt a holiday

METHOD 6

When one sentence is negative and the other sentence is affirmative, we can combine them in another way.

EXAMPLE   John is from Boston.   Bill isn't from Boston.
<u>John is from Boston but Bill isn't.</u> or <u>Bill isn't from Boston but John is.</u>

EXERCISE *In the space provided, combine each pair of sentences into one sentence, using method 6. Add all necessary punctuation.*

1. the book is expensive   the notebook isnt expensive

2. thomas smith is teaching now annette ford isnt teaching now

3. the chairs are new   the desk isnt new

1. the eggs arent in the regrigerator   the milk is in the refrigerator

2. george harris isnt a french teacher   albert dubois is a french teacher

3. the sofa isnt comfortable   the bed is comfortable

EXERCISE   *In the space provided, combine each pair of sentences into one sentence, using method 4, 5, or 6.*

1. beethoven is a composer   mozart is a composer

2. potatoes are vegetables   apples arent vegetables

3. the lights are on   the radio isnt on

4. the dormitory isnt a new building   the library is a new building

5. spinach is a vegetable   corn is a vegetable

6. boston isnt a state   chicago isnt a state

PART II
Model Paragraph

The Students in the Class

Maria is Latin American and Joao is too. Joao is Brazilian but Maria isn't. Erika is a blonde and Helga is too. Dr. Chen isn't European and Joseph Lacroix isn't either. Michael and Dimitrios are Europeans and Pierre and Klaus are too.

Copy the following paragraph. Fill in the blanks with the names of people in your class or of people you know, and with facts about them.

(name)   (name)

_____ is _____ and _____ is too.

   (name)   (name)

_____ and _____ are _____

      (name)   (name)

and _____ is too. _____ isn't _____

      (name)   (name)   (name)

and _____ isn't either. _____ and _____

                    (name)   (name)

are _____ but _____ and _____ aren't.

LESSON 9
The Article I

The Indefinite and Definite Article

THE INDEFINITE ARTICLE

The indefinite article is a before a singular noun beginning with a consonant sound and an before a singular noun beginning with a vowel sound.

EXAMPLE   There is a book on the table.
                There is an apple on the table.

A and an are not used before uncountable nouns.

EXAMPLE: There is sugar on the table.

A and an have no plural form.

EXAMPLE   There are books on the table.
                There are apples on the table.

The word some can be used before uncountable nouns and countable nouns in the plural.

EXAMPLE   There is some sugar on the table.
                There are some books on the table.
                There are some apples on the table.

EXERCISE   *In the space provided, copy the following sentences, putting a, an, or some in place of the blanks. Add all necessary punctuation.*

    1. im drinking _____ coffee

    2. im reading _____ book

    3. im buying _____ shirts

    4. johns studying _____ english book

5. marys buying _____ new dress

6. teds singing _____ old song

7. ellens talking to _____ old friends

THE DEFINITE ARTICLE

The definite article is <u>the</u>. It has several uses in English. We are going to
study two of them now. The definite article is used with <u>unique</u> and
<u>identified</u> things.

EXAMPLE   There is <u>a</u> book on <u>the</u> table.   <u>The</u> book is new.

The table in the first sentence is unique. It may be the only table in the
room. At least, it is the only table the speaker of the sentence is speaking
about. In the second sentence the book is identified. The speaker
identified it in the previous sentence, so it changes from <u>a</u> book to <u>the</u>
book.

EXAMPLE   There is a pen in my hand.   <u>The</u> pen is red.

Again, we say <u>the pen</u> in the second sentence, because it is not only
<u>a pen,</u> it is the same pen that is in the first sentence. It is now
identified.

EXAMPLE   There are two windows in the room.   <u>The</u> windows are open.

The windows are identified and unique. How?

EXERCISE   *In the space provided, copy these sentences and put either
a, an, the, or some in the blank spaces. Add all necessary
punctuation.*

1. there is _____ hat on Janes head _____ hat is pretty

2. there is _____ girl in _____ first seat _____ girl is pretty

3. there is _____ sign on _____ wall _____ sign is large

4. there is _____ man in this picture _____ man is handsome

_____

1. there are _____ pictures on my wall _____ pictures are pretty

2. there are _____ pens in johns pocket _____ pens are red

3. there are _____ cats in the living room _____ cats are crying

4. there are _____ cookies in that jar _____ cookies are delicious

_____

1. there is _____ coffee in this pot _____ coffee is hot

2. there is _____ beer in my refrigerator _____ beer is cold

3. there is _____ candy in my pocket _____ candy is good

PART II
Model Paragraph

Mrs. Brown is working in her kitchen. She is working at a large table. There is a bowl on the table. There are some eggs on the table. There is a bag of flour on the table. There is a carton of milk on the table. There is some butter in the bowl. Mrs. Brown is mixing the butter and the sugar together and adding the flour and the eggs. What is Mrs. Brown making?

EXERCISE *Cover the Model Paragraph with a piece of paper. Copy the following paragraph. Fill in the blanks with a, an, the, or some. Add all necessary punctuation.*

mrs brown is working in her kitchen she is working at _____ large

table there is _____ bowl on _____ table there are _____

eggs on _____ table there is _____ box of flour on _____

table there is _____ carton of milk on _____ table there is

_____ butter in _____ bowl mrs brown is mixing _____

butter and _____ sugar together and adding _____ flour and

_____ eggs what is mrs brown making

LESSON 10
The Article II

PART I
Expression of Quantity

When we write sentences in question or negative form, we use <u>a</u> or <u>an</u> only with *singular countable* nouns as we do in statements.

EXAMPLE   There is <u>a</u> book on the table.
Is there <u>a</u> book on the table?
There isn't <u>a</u> book on the table.

EXERCISE   *In the space provided, change each sentence to a question and copy it. Add all necessary punctuation.*

    1. there is a bottle of milk in robert wards refrigerator

    2. there is a radio in the corner

    3. there is a post office in the neighborhood

    4. there is a pillow on the bed

EXERCISE   *In the space provided, copy the same sentences, but change them to **negative** sentences.*

    1.

    2.

    3.

    4.

We can also express the idea of nonexistence by using the adjective <u>no.</u> To understand this use of <u>no,</u> think of it as a number equivalent to zero.

EXAMPLE   There is a book on the table. (one book)
There is <u>no</u> table in the classroom. (zero books)

In the space provided, change the following sentences to negative sentences using no. *Add all necessary punctuation.*

1. there is a chair in the bedroom

2. there is a dishwasher in mrs allens kitchen

3. there is a cafeteria in the main building

4. there is an umbrella in the closet

When we make questions with plural countable nouns we often use the word any to ask about quantity, in the same way that we use some in affirmative sentences. We sometimes use some in questions also, but in this lesson we will practice the use of any. Some is never used in negative statements.

EXAMPLE There are some apples in the bowl.
Are there any apples in the bowl?
There aren't any apples in the bowl.

EXERCISE *In the space provided, change the following statements to questions, changing* some *to* any. *Add all necessary punctuation.*

1. there are some students in the hall

2. there are some pictures on mr dales bedroom wall

3. there are some new stores on main street

4. there are some eggs in the refrigerator

EXERCISE *In the space provided, change the four sentences above to negative sentences and copy.*

1.

2.

3.

4.

We can also use no with plural, countable nouns.

EXAMPLE There are five apples in the bowl. (five apples)
There are no apples in the bowl.   (zero apples)

EXERCISE *In the space provided, change the following sentences to negative sentences with* no. *Add all necessary punctuation.*

1. there are some children in mrs hubbards house

2. there are two books on the table

3. there are some cups in the kitchen cabinet

4. there are some good programs on television tonight

We also normally change <u>some</u> to <u>any</u> with noncountable nouns.

EXAMPLE   There is <u>some</u> milk in the glass.
Is there <u>any</u> milk in the glass?
There isn't <u>any</u> milk in the glass.

EXERCISE   *In the space provided, change the following statements to questions. Add all necessary punctuation.*

1. there is some dirt on the window

2. there is some coffee on toms shirt

3. there is some water in the dogs dish

4. there is some mustard on this hamburger

EXERCISE   *In the space provided, change the same sentences to negative statements.*

1.

2.

3.

4.

We can also use <u>no</u> with noncountable nouns.

EXERCISE   *In the space provided, change the following sentences into negative sentences, using <u>no</u>. Add all necessary punctuation.*

1. there is some food on the table

2. there is some wine in pierres glass

3. there is some snow on the ground

4. there is some ice in the freezer

Practice Composition

Copy the following composition, putting words of your own in the blank spaces:

My Home

     in my home there is a _____ and a _____ there are some _____ and some _____. there is a _____ but there is no _____ and there are no _____. There isnt any _____ and there isnt any _____ either. im happy in my home with my _____, my _____, and my _____.

(singular countable)   (plural countable)   (uncountable)

LESSON 11
The Habitual Present Tense

Verbs in the habitual present tense add -s in the third person.

EXAMPLE   I eat breakfast every morning.
John eats breakfast every morning.

EXERCISE   *In the space provided, change the subject of each sentence below to John. Add all necessary punctuation.*

1. i read the newspaper every morning

2. i write to my family every week

3. i listen to the radio every night

4. i take a shower every morning

Verbs that end in -s, -z, -ch, -sh, -x add -es.

EXAMPLE   I dress every morning.
John dresses every morning.

EXERCISE   *In the space provided, change the subject of each sentence from I to Mr. Harris and copy. Add all necessary punctuation.*

1. i watch television every night

2. i cross the street at the corner

3. i brush my shoes

4. i teach the dog to sit up

5. i wash the breakfast dishes every morning

Verbs ending in -o takes -es.

EXAMPLE   I go to Miami in winter.
John goes to Miami in winter.

EXERCISE   *In the space provided, change the subject of each sentence from I to Mary and copy. Add all necessary punctuation.*

1. i do the homework

2. i go to church on sunday

3. i do the dishes every night

4. i go to bed early on school nights

Verbs that end in -y with a *consonant* before change the -y to ie in the third person.

EXAMPLE   I study every day.
John studies every day.

EXERCISE   *In the space provided, change the subject of each sentence from I to Juan and copy. Add all necessary punctuation.*

1. i try to speak english

2. i study the new words

3. i carry the books to school

4. i worry about my job

5. i hurry home after school

Verbs that end in -y with a *vowel* before add *only* -s.

EXAMPLE   I play the piano
John plays the piano.

EXERCISE   *In the space provided, change the subject of each sentence from I to Mr. Ford and copy. Add all necessary punctuation.*

1. i buy a sandwich for lunch

2. i play cards every night

3. i enjoy television

4. i stay home when it rains

5. i play soccer on weekends

In the space provided, change the subject of each sentence from I to Mary and copy. Add all necessary punctuation.

1. i study every night

2. i play baseball in warm weather

3. i stay in school until four oclock

4. i try to pass all my tests

5. i buy a newspaper every morning

6. i fly to europe every summer

The verb have changes to has in the third person.

EXAMPLE
I have two brothers.
John has two brothers.

EXERCISE *In the space provided, change the subject of each sentence from I to George and copy. Add all necessary punctuation.*

1. i have a large apartment

2. i have a lot of books

3. i have parties on saturday nights

4. i have friends in california

5. i have three children

EXERCISE *In the space provided, change the subject of each sentence from I to Mrs. Green and copy. Make any other necessary changes and add all necessary punctuation.*

1. i sit in the front row

2. i cry at sad movies

3. i have a persian cat

4. i dress warmly in winter

5. i buy christmas presents

6. i wash my windows every week

7. i have new shoes

8. i play cards with my friends

9. i pronounce english words carefully

10. i try to understand the teacher

PART II
Model Paragraph

Copy the following paragraph, changing the subject from I to Carlos in the first sentence and to he in the following sentences. Add all necessary punctuation.

i get up at seven oclock every morning, take a shower and brush my teeth then i dress and get my breakfast for breakfast i make a cup of coffee fry two eggs and fix two pieces of toast after i have breakfast i study my lesson for the day or i watch television at eight oclock i leave the house and take the subway to school

LESSON 12
The Indefinite Pronoun

PART I
Singular and Plural Indefinite Pronouns

With identified nouns (see Lesson Eight) that do not refer to persons, we use <u>it</u> as a pronoun in the singular.

EXAMPLE   John likes the book.   I like the book too.
                     John likes the book.   I like <u>it</u> too.

With unidentified nouns that do not refer to persons, we use <u>one</u> as a pronoun in the singular.

EXAMPLE   John is reading a book.   I'm reading a book too.
                     John is reading a book.   I'm reading <u>one</u> too.

EXERCISE   *In the space provided, copy the sentences below, putting <u>one</u> in place of the underlined words. Add all necessary punctuation.*

1. im buying a tie   george is buying <u>a tie</u> too

2. im eating an apple   sally is eating <u>an apple</u> too

3. bill is having a party   tom is having <u>a party</u> too

With identified nouns in the plural, we use <u>they</u> or <u>them</u> as pronouns.

EXAMPLE   I like these books.   Tom likes these books, too.
                     I like these books.   Tom likes <u>them</u>, too.
                     The apples are big.   The apples are red, too.
                     The apples are big.   <u>They</u> are red, too.

With unidentified nouns in the plural, we use <u>some</u> as a pronoun.

EXAMPLE   I'm buying some shirts.   Tom is buying some shirts too.
                     I'm buying some shirts.   Tom is buying <u>some</u> too.

EXERCISE   *In the space provided, copy these sentences, putting <u>some</u> in place of the underlined words. Add all necessary punctuation.*

1. im reading some books   tom is reading <u>some books</u> too

2. mary is baking some cookies   harry is baking <u>some cookies</u> too

3. ed has some peanuts   joe has <u>some peanuts</u> too

EXERCISE   *In the space provided, copy these sentences, putting <u>one</u> or <u>some</u> in place of the underlined words. Add all necessary punctuation.*

1. im looking at a book and tom is looking at <u>a book</u> too

2. im reading some stories and joe is reading <u>some stories</u> too

3. im frying some eggs and betsy is frying <u>some eggs</u> too

4. im eating a banana and anna is eating <u>a banana</u> too

EXERCISE   *In the space provided, copy these sentences, putting <u>one</u>, <u>some</u>, <u>it</u>, or <u>them</u> in place of the underlined words. Add all necessary punctuation.*

1. im washing some clothes   alice is washing <u>some clothes</u> too

2. im copying the words   alice is copying <u>the words</u> too

3. im studying the lesson   june is studying <u>the lesson</u> too

4. im drinking some coffee   the girls are drinking <u>some coffee</u> too

5. im baking a cake   mrs williams is baking <u>a cake</u> too

Note: **One is not used after a *possessive*.**

EXAMPLE   My car is red.   John's car is blue.
          My car is red.   <u>John's</u> is blue.

One is also not used after a *number*.

EXAMPLE   John eats two eggs for breakfast.   Bill eats three eggs.
          John eats two eggs for breakfast.   Bill eats <u>three.</u>

54

EXERCISE   *In the space provided, copy each sentence, putting the*
correct number in place of the underlined words. Add all
necessary punctuation.

1. john has two brothers   i have <u>three brothers</u>

2. johns apartment has four rooms   mine has <u>three rooms</u>

3. mr brown has two cars   i have only <u>one car</u>

**We can use <u>one</u> with an identified noun in the following case. Study
the examples.**

EXAMPLE   The book on the table is mine.   The book on the chair is John's.
The book on the table is mine.   The <u>one</u> on the chair is John's.
The red car is mine.   The blue car is John's.
The red car is mine.   The blue <u>one</u> is John's

EXERCISE   *In the space provided, copy these sentences, putting <u>one</u> in*
place of the underlined word. Add all necessary punctuation.

1. the new building is a hospital   the old <u>building</u> is a school

2. the kitchen in your apartment is large the <u>kitchen</u> in my apartment is small

3. the blue book is a grammar book   the red <u>book</u> is a dictionary

4. the window in the living room is open   the <u>window</u> in the bedroom is closed

**When we use <u>one</u> in this way, it has a plural form, <u>ones.</u> Study the
examples.**

EXAMPLE   The books on the table are mine.   The books on the chairs are Tom's.
The books on the table are mine.   The <u>ones</u> on the table are Tom's.
I'm buying two green ties.   John's buying two red ties.
I'm buying two green ties.   John's buying two red <u>ones.</u>

EXERCISE   *In the space provided, copy these sentences, putting <u>ones</u>*
in place of the underlined word.

1. the exercises in lesson five are difficult   the <u>exercises</u> in lesson six are easy

2. the chairs in this room are comfortable   the <u>chairs</u> in that room are uncomfortable

3. the classrooms on the tenth floor are   the <u>classrooms</u> on the third floor are small
pleasant   and dark

4. there are three old books on the chair   there are three new <u>books</u> on the table

I have a brother in New York and a brother in California. The one in California is tall. The one in New York is short. The tall one is handsome, but the short one is fat. The one in California has three cars, a small red one and two big black ones. The red one is a sports car, but the other ones are not. My brother drives the red one and one of the black ones. He keeps the third one for extra parts.

EXERCISE   *Cover the Model Paragraph with a piece of paper. Copy the following paragraph, putting* <u>one</u> *or* <u>ones</u> *in place of the underlined words. Add all necessary punctuation.*

i have a brother in new york and a brother in california the <u>brother</u> in california is tall the <u>brother</u> in new york is <u>short</u> the tall <u>brother</u> is handsome but the short <u>brother</u> is fat the <u>brother</u> in california has three cars a small red <u>car</u> and two big black <u>cars</u> the red <u>car</u> is a sports car but the other <u>cars</u> are not my brother drives the red <u>car</u> and one of the black <u>cars</u> he keeps the other <u>car</u> for extra parts

LESSON 13A
Sequence of Events

PART I
Before, After, and Afterward

BEFORE

When we talk about two events, we can show which event happened
first and which happened second by using the words before and after.

EXAMPLE   I put on my glasses.   I read the paper.

Method 1: I put on my glasses before I read the paper.
Method 2: Before I read the paper, I put on my glasses.

EXERCISE   *In the space provided, make each pair of sentences into one
sentence, using before. Use method 1.*

1. I wake up.   I get up.

2. I wash.   I get dressed.

3. I get dressed.   I eat breakfast.

4. I read the paper.   I leave the house.

EXERCISE   *In the space provided, repeat the last exercise, using
method 2.*

1.

2.

3.

4.

AFTER

EXAMPLE   Method 1:   I read the paper <u>after</u> I put on my glasses.
                         <u>After</u> I put on my glasses, I read the paper.

Note: **Notice the comma in method 2 sentences.**

EXERCISE   *In the space provided, make each pair of sentences into one, using <u>after</u>. Use method 1.*

1. I leave the house.   I put on my coat.

2. I wait for the bus.   I get to the bus stop.

3. I put my fare in the box.   I get on the bus.

4. I go to sleep.   I sit down.

EXERCISE   *In the spaces provided, repeat the last exercise, using method 2.*

1.

2.

3.

4.

AFTERWARD

Notice that <u>after</u> is used with the *first* event. Another word, <u>afterward</u>, is used with the *second* event. Study the example.

EXAMPLE   After I put on my glasses, I read the paper.

                Method 1:   I put on my glasses. I read the paper <u>afterward</u>.
                Method 2:   I put on my glasses. <u>Afterward</u>, I read the paper.

Note the commas in the method 2 example. Also note that afterward does *not* make two sentences into one.

EXERCISE   *In the space provided, copy each pair of sentences and add <u>afterward</u> to the second sentence, following method 1.*

1. Peter does his homework.   He watches television.

2. George watches television until ten o'clock.   He has a snack.

3. The Carters have dinner at a restaurant on   They go dancing.
    Saturdays.

58

EXERCISE *In the space provided, repeat the last exercise, using method 2.*

1.

2.

3.

THE -ING FORM

We can make the sentences above simpler by using the -ing form of the verb. Study the examples.

EXAMPLE I put on my glasses before I read the paper.
I put on my glasses before reading the paper.
After I put on my glasses, I read the paper.
After putting on my glasses, I read the paper.

EXERCISE *In the space provided, copy the following sentences, changing the phrases that follow before or after to -ing phrases.*

1. I study my homework before I come to class.

2. I do my homework before I go to bed.

3. I put sugar in my coffee before I drink it.

4. After I take my shower, I go to bed.

5. After I write to my family, I take a nap.

6. After I change my clothes, I work in the garden.

PART II
Model Paragraphs

Every summer I go to the beach for two weeks. Before I go, I make a hotel reservation by mail. Before I mail the letter, I make sure it has a stamp on it. The night before I leave, I pack my bag. Before I get on the train, I buy my ticket at the railroad station.

After I arrive at the beach, I take a taxi to the hotel. After I get to my hotel room, I unpack my bag and get ready to go swimming. After I put on my bathing suit, I put suntan lotion on my skin.

Copy the model paragraphs and change the underlined phrases to -ing phrases.

LESSON 13B
Sequence of Events

PART III
Before, After, and the -ing Phrase

EXERCISE *In the space provided, combine each pair of sentences into one by using <u>before</u>. Use method 1.*

1. I pick up my books.   I go to the subway station.

2. I buy a token.   I get on the subway.

3. I study my lesson.   I get off the train.

EXERCISE *In the space provided, combine the pairs of sentences in the last exercise into one sentence by using <u>after</u>. Use method 1.*

1.

2.

3.

EXERCISE *In the space provided, copy the sentences in the last exercise, and change the phrase beginning with <u>after</u> into an <u>-ing</u> phrase.*

1.

2.

3.

Mr. Brown's Morning

Mr. Brown wakes up at 6:30 after his alarm clock rings. He washes and shaves before dressing. After he dresses, he fries two eggs and makes a pot of coffee. He reads the morning paper before putting on his hat and coat. After he puts on his hat and coat, he walks to his car. He drives for half an hour before arriving at his office. After he arrives there, he puts his car in a garage and goes to work.

FREE COMPOSITION

My Morning

LESSON 14A
Combining Sentences III

BECAUSE

We use the word *because* to join two sentences when the second sentence shows the cause of the first sentence.

EXAMPLE   I'm washing the dishes.   They're dirty.
I'm washing the dishes <u>because</u> they're dirty.

EXERCISE   *In the space provided, make each pair of sentences into one sentence by using <u>because</u>.*

1. I'm going to bed.   I'm tired.

2. I'm going to the doctor.   I feel sick.

3. I'm making a sandwich.   I'm hungry.

4. I'm opening a bottle of milk.   I'm thirsty.

5. I'm putting on a sweater.   I feel cold.

SO

We use *so* to join two sentences when the first sentence shows the cause of the second sentence.

EXAMPLE   The dishes are dirty.   I'm washing them.
The dishes are dirty <u>so</u> I'm washing them.

EXERCISE
*In the space provided, make the sentences in the last exercise into one sentence by using so. Put the **second** sentence first.*

1. I'm tired so

2.

3.

4.

5.

EXERCISE
In the space provided, make each pair of sentences into a single sentence, using because.

1. My feet hurt.   My shoes are tight.

2. My eyes hurt.   The light is bad.

3. I'm very unhappy.   My office is cold.

4. The baby is crying.   His stomach is empty.

5. I can't sleep.   The baby is crying.

EXAMPLE   The room is cold.   I'm opening the window.
I'm opening the window <u>because</u> the room is cold.
The room is cold <u>so</u> I'm opening the window.

EXERCISE
In the space provided, make each pair of sentences into one sentence, using because and so.

1. It's a hot day.   I'm making lemonade.

   1. _____ because _____.

   2. _____ so _____.

2. I can't hear you.   The radio is too loud.

   1. _____ because _____.

   2. _____ so _____.

3. I'm turning on the television.   I want to hear the news.

   1. _____ because _____.

   2. _____ so _____.

64

SENTENCES AND NOUN PHRASES

Here is a way to make a sentence into a noun phrase.

EXAMPLE   The dishes are dirty.   the dirty dishes

After we make a sentence into a noun phrase, we can make it part of another sentence.

EXAMPLE   The dirty dishes are in the sink.
            I'm washing the dirty dishes.

EXERCISE   *In the space provided, change these sentences to noun phrases. You will see that they are the second sentences from the last exercise.*

1. My shoes are tight.   my _____

2. The light is bad.   the _____

3. My coffee is cold.   my _____

4. His stomach is empty.   his _____

5. The baby is crying.   the _____

If we use a noun phrase to show the cause in a because sentence, we change the because to because of.

EXAMPLE   My feet hurt because my shoes are tight.
            My feet hurt because of my tight shoes.

EXERCISE   *In the space provided, change the following sentences from sentences with because to sentences with because of.*

1. I am uncomfortable because the room is warm.

2. Sally is popular because her hair is blond.

3. Lucy is unpopular because her voice is loud.

4. Everybody is laughing because the clown is funny.

Someday I want to visit California because <u>the weather is wonderful.</u>
I want to see San Francisco because <u>the cable cars are funny</u> and <u>the
houses are old.</u> I want to visit Los Angeles because <u>the streets are wide</u>
and <u>the hotels are modern.</u> And finally, I want to go to Big Sur because
<u>the beach is wide</u> and <u>the scenery is beautiful.</u>

EXERCISE   *Copy the model paragraph. Change each <u>because</u> to <u>because</u>
<u>of</u> and each underlined clause to a noun phrase.*

LESSON 14B
Combining Sentences III

PART III
Because, So, and Noun Phrases

EXERCISE *In the space provided, make each pair of sentences into one sentence, using* because.

1. I'm enjoying the concert.   The music is beautiful.

2. I'm lonely.   My friend is out of town.

3. This fruit salad is delicious.   The fruit is fresh.

4. I like this book.   The story is interesting.

5. I like this exercise.   The words are easy.

EXERCISE *In the space provided, make the sentences in the last exercise into one sentence, using* so. *Put the second sentence first.*

1. The music is beautiful, so

2.

3.

4.

5.

Name _____ *Date* _____   **67**

EXERCISE   *In the space provided, change the following sentences into noun phrases.*

1. The water is hot.   the _____

2. The girl is tall.   the _____

3. The book is expensive.   the _____

EXERCISE   *In the space provided, change these sentences with* <u>because</u> *to sentences with* <u>because of.</u>

1. I like this book because the pictures are beautiful.

2. I like Maria because her conversation is interesting.

3. I like this restaurant because the food is cheap.

PART IV
Model Paragraph

New York is my city. I like it because of its busy streets and its tall buildings. I like it because its neighborhoods are colorful and exciting. I like Greenwich Village because of its funny little houses and interesting people. I like the East Side because it has many boutiques and movie theaters. I like the theater district because of its bright electric signs. And I like my little apartment because it's mine.

FREE COMPOSITION

My City

The past form of regular verbs ends in -ed.

EXAMPLE I walk to school every day.
I <u>walked</u> to school yesterday.

EXERCISE *In the space provided, change each of the following sentences to the past form by changing the verb and the time expression to show past time.*

1. I wash and dress every morning.

2. I clean my apartment every day.

3. I watch television every night.

4. I walk home every day.

5. My dog barks at me every day.

When a verb ends in y with a consonant before it, the y changes to ie in the past.

EXAMPLE I study my lesson every night.
I <u>studied</u> my lesson last night.

1. The babies cry every morning.

2. I try to answer the teacher's questions every morning.

3. I carry my books to school every day.

4. I hurry home after class every day.

5. I copy the sentences every day.

Name _____ Date _____   **71**

When a verb ends in y with a *vowel* before it, the y does not change.

EXAMPLE I play tennis every week.
I played tennis last week.

EXERCISE *In the space provided, change each of the following sentences to the past form by changing the verb and the time expression to show past time.*

    1. I enjoy lunch with my friends every day.

    2. I stay home every Sunday.

    3. My parents pray every night.

    4. My friends and I play soccer on weekends.

EXERCISE *In the space provided, change each of the following sentences to the past form by changing the verb and the time expression to show past time (see Lesson Five).*

    1. I try to get home early every day.

    2. My little sister plays with her dolls every day.

    3. I stay inside after dark.

    4. I carry my lunch to school with me.

    5. I enjoy meeting my friends after school.

When a verb ends in a consonant with a vowel before, we usually double the consonant before we add -ed.

EXAMPLE I stop working at five o'clock every day.
I stopped working at five o'clock yesterday.

    1. I (drop) my book on the floor.

    2. The salesperson (wrap) my package.

    3. The rabbit (hop) across the field.

    4. The dancer (pin) a rose in her hair.

    5. I (drag) the heavy chair across the room.

When a word of *more than one syllable* ends in a consonant with a vowel before, and the final syllable is *not accented,* we do not double the consonant (see Lesson Five).

The teacher <u>enters</u> the classroom at ten o'clock every morning.
The teacher <u>entered</u> the classroom at ten o'clock yesterday morning.

EXERCISE *In the space provided, copy the following sentences, putting the verb in parentheses in the past form.*

1. I (travel) to Florida on my vacation.

2. I (water) my plants this morning.

3. The store (deliver) a package to my house.

4. I (remember) my sister's birthday last week.

EXERCISE *In the space provided, copy the following sentences, putting the verb in parentheses in the past form.*

1. The tired child (bother) his mother.

2. The people (clap) when the speaker finished.

3. I (stop) my car at the red light.

4. Mr. Baker (travel) to Mexico last summer.

When a verb ends in an <u>e</u> that is not pronounced, we add only <u>-d</u> to the verb.

EXAMPLE I <u>bake</u> cookies every weekend.
I <u>baked</u> cookies last weekend.

EXERCISE *In the space provided, copy the following sentences, putting the verb in parentheses in the past form.*

1. I (live) in Cairo as a child.

2. My grandfather (smoke) big cigars.

3. I (decide) to go to bed early last night.

4. The guitarist (tune) his guitar.

EXERCISE *In the space provided, copy the following sentences, putting the verb in parentheses in the past form.*

1. Mary (play) the piano at the party.

2. I (dream) about my family last night.

3. I (stop) reading at eleven o'clock last night.

4. The cat (chase) the dog.

5. I (study) my lessons carefully yesterday.

6. Ellen Smith (bake) a chocolate cake.

7. The big dog (frighten) the child.

8. The fire (destroy) the house.

9. John (marry) a beautiful girl.

10. I (rap) on the door.

11. The new students (register) for the course.

12. I (want) to be a cowboy when I was a child.

PART II
Exercise Paragraph

Copy the following paragraph, putting the verbs in parentheses in the past form.

Mehmet (live) in Turkey, but he (want) to come to the United States to study English. He (ask) his English teacher and his teacher said "I (study) English last summer at a school in Los Angeles. I (learn) a lot there, and I think you will, too." Mehmet (decide) to go to that school, so he (address) a letter to the school and (drop) it in the mailbox. Two weeks later, the school (reply). They (accept) him as a student. Later that year, Mehmet (travel) to California and (stay) there for a year.

LESSON 15B
The Regular Past Tense

PART III
-ed, ied, Doubling the Consonant

EXERCISE   *In the space provided, copy the following sentences, putting the verb in parentheses in the past form.*

1. John (play) tennis with Mary last Saturday.

2. We (enjoy) our breakfast this morning.

3. I (carry) the groceries home yesterday afternoon.

4. I (stay) home last night.

5. The babies (cry) for their bottles last night.

6. Professor Jones (marry) Mrs. Jones ten years ago.

7. The students (worry) about the exam yesterday.

8. The storm (destroy) the beach house.

9. I (try) to call you last night.

10. The talking students (annoy) the teacher.

EXERCISE   *In the space provided, copy the following sentences, putting the verb in parentheses in the past form.*

1. I (talk) to my advisor yesterday.

2. I (study) for the test last week.

3. I (live) in Texas as a child.

Name _____ *Date* _____   **75**

4. I (enjoy) my dinner last night.

5. I (wash) my car yesterday.

6. I (stay) home last night.

7. My father (smoke) a pipe.

8. I (listen) to an opera on the radio last night.

9. I (stop) reading at ten o'clock last night.

10. I (play) chess with my brother last night.

11. I (travel) to Jamaica on my vacation.

12. I (race) my brother to the corner.

13. I (drop) my pencil on the floor.

14. I (open) my book to page three.

15. I (worry) about the test last week.

16. I (paint) my apartment last week.

17. Maria (tap) on the door.

18. I (carry) the groceries home yesterday.

PART IV
Model Paragraph

This is how John Brown and his wife Mary <u>passed</u> the weekend. On Friday night, the Browns <u>visited</u> their friends the Walkers, and they all <u>played</u> cards. They <u>enjoyed</u> the evening, but it was late when they <u>arrived</u> home. The next morning Mary Brown was tired, so John Brown <u>prepared</u> breakfast. After breakfast, he <u>looked</u> at the morning paper for a few minutes, then he <u>worked</u> in the garden until lunchtime. In the afternoon, he <u>watched</u> a football game on television. Mary Brown <u>shopped</u> for groceries at the same time. In the evening, they <u>looked</u> at photographs from their last vacation. They <u>stayed</u> up late and <u>talked</u> about their trip. On Sunday they <u>rested</u> most of the day, but in the evening, John <u>corrected</u> homework papers, and Mary <u>baked</u> bread.

FREE COMPOSITION

Use at least five of the following verbs in the past form: pass, visit, play, enjoy, arrive, prepare, look, work, watch, shop, stay, talk, rest, correct, bake.

My Weekend

LESSON 16A
The Past Tense of Irregular Verbs

PART I
Changes in Spelling and Vowel Sounds

Some irregular verbs have irregular past forms. It is difficult to make rules for these verbs, but we can describe a few general categories. Some irregular verbs change only the vowels when they change to the past.

EXAMPLE   I <u>come</u> to school every day.
              I <u>came</u> to school yesterday.

Other verbs in this category are these:

Present	*Past*
find	found
get	got
take	took
see	saw
eat	ate
write	wrote
wake	woke
fall	fell

EXERCISE   *In the space provided, copy the following sentences, putting the verb in parentheses in the past form.*

1. I (stand) when the teacher (come) into the room.

2. I (find) a quarter on the sidewalk.

3. I (get) a present for my mother's birthday.

4. I (take) a taxi to school this morning.

5. I (see) a good movie last night.

6. I (write) my homework last night.

7. I (eat) a big breakfast this morning.

8. I (wake) up early today.

9. My books (fall) off the table.

Another group of irregular verbs has a d in the present form that changes to t in the past.

EXAMPLE   I send a letter to my family every week.
                I sent a letter to my family yesterday.

Other verbs in this category are these:

Present	*Past*
build	built
bend	bent
lend	lent
spend	spent

EXERCISE   *In the space provided, copy each sentence, putting the verb in parentheses in the past form.*

1. I (build) a house for my dog.

2. I (send) my shirts to the laundry.

3. My roommate (lend) me five dollars.

4. I (spend) ten dollars at the supermarket today.

5. The tall man (bend) down to enter the room.

Another group of irregular verbs has both a vowel change and a final t.

EXAMPLE   I bring my lunch to school every day.
                I brought my lunch to school yesterday.

The verb in this example has a gh in the past form. Other gh verbs are these:

Present	*Past*
teach	taught
catch	caught
buy	bought
think	thought

EXERCISE   *In the space provided, copy the following sentences, putting the verb in parentheses in the past form.*

1. The teacher (teach) us some new words yesterday.

2. I (buy) new shoes yesterday.

3. The child (catch) the ball.

4. I (think) about my family last night.

5. The mail carrier (bring) me a letter from home.

Another group of verbs in this category changes the vowel sound and the spelling of the vowel from two letters to one.

EXAMPLE   I <u>feel</u> tired every night.
I <u>felt</u> tired last night.

Other verbs in this group are these:

Present	*Past*
keep	kept
leave	left
sleep	slept

EXERCISE   *In the space provided, copy each sentence, putting the verb in parentheses in the past form.*

1. I (keep) my windows closed during the storm.

2. I (leave) home at eight o'clock this morning.

3. I (sleep) eight hours last night.

4. I (feel) happy when I finished my work.

Another group of verbs *does not change its form at all* in the past.

EXAMPLE   My mother <u>cuts</u> the bread for dinner.
My mother <u>cut</u> the bread last night.

Other verbs in this category are these:

Present	*Past*
cut	cut
hit	hit
hurt	hurt

Note: **The verb <u>read</u> changes only pronunciation in the past form.**

In the space provided, copy the following sentences, putting the verb in parentheses in the past form.

    1. John (hurt) his leg in an auto accident.

    2. Mary (cut) her finger with a knife.

    3. John (hit) the baseball hard.

    4. Mary (put) cream in her coffee.

    5. I (read) an interesting story in the newspaper.

A few irregular verbs do not fit easily into any category:

EXAMPLE   I am tired today.   We are tired today.
                   I was tired yesterday.   We were tired yesterday.

Other such verbs are these:

Present	*Past*
have	had
go	went

EXERCISE   *In the space provided, copy the following sentences, putting the verb in parentheses in the past form.*

    1. I (have) a good time at the party.

    2. I (go) to a dance last night.

    3. The students (be) all in class yesterday.

EXERCISE   *In the space provided, copy the following sentences, putting the verbs in parentheses in the past form.*

    1. I (spend) all my money at the circus.

    2. I (stand) on the corner and waited for the bus.

    3. I (bring) some sandwiches for the picnic.

    4. I (feel) happy when I passed the test.

    5. I (put) on my coat when I (go) outside.

    6. I (buy) a bracelet for Christina.

    7. Bill (hurt) his hand playing baseball.

8. Alicia (leave) the party early.

9. Miguel (be) tired after the soccer game.

10. My parents (send) me some money.

11. The teacher (come) to class early.

12. Ahmed (take) Yoshiko to the movies.

13. Mary (get) a new handbag.

14. Albert Gray (go) to Hawaii last summer.

15. Mr. Jones (build) a cabinet for his workshop.

16. Felipe (fall) down and (hit) his head.

17. I (sleep) badly last night.

18. I (teach) my little brother to tie his shoes.

*In the space provided, copy the following paragraph, putting the verbs
in parentheses in the past form.*

Bill's Terrible Morning

Bill (wake) up at seven o'clock. He (feel) very sleepy. There (be) no
hot water for washing, and when he shaved he (cut) his face. When he
(come) downstairs, he (eat) a breakfast of cold scrambled eggs and
burned toast with cold coffee. When he (get) outside, it was raining. He
waited fifteen minutes but no taxis (come). Finally he (take) a bus but
it was crowded so he (stand) all the way to the office. What a terrible
way to begin the day!

LESSON 16B
The Past Tense of Irregular Verbs

PART III
Changes in Spelling and Vowel Sounds

EXERCISE   *In the space provided, copy the following sentences, putting the verb in parentheses in the past form.*

1. Spring (come) early this year.

2. I (stand) in line at the bank for half an hour.

3. John (find) the word in his dictionary.

4. We played soccer until we (get) tired.

5. I (take) an aspirin for my headache.

6. I (see) the new show at the museum.

7. Frank (write) a poem for his friend.

8. The alarm clock (wake) me at six o'clock.

9. My little sister (fall) out of bed last night.

10. Mr. Garcia (send) his son to the grocery store.

11. I (build) a garage in my yard.

12. I (bend) over and picked up my book.

13. I (lend) my book to Tomas.

14. I (spend) ten dollars for a ticket to a concert.

15. Vladimir (bring) his friend to class.

16. George Wilson (teach) in Brazil for two years.

17. I (buy) an ice cream cone after lunch.

18. The baseball player (catch) the ball in his glove.

19. I (think) about my home last week.

20. We all (feel) tired after the dance.

21. I (keep) my windows open last night.

22. I (leave) my books home today.

23. Willem (sleep) all day last Sunday.

24. I (put) my homework on the teacher's desk.

25. I (cut) the bread for dinner.

26. The car (hit) a tree.

27. Pierre (hurt) his ankle when he (fall) on the ice.

28. My friends (be) all at the dance last night.

29. I (have) a delicious steak for dinner last night.

30. I (go) directly home after class yesterday.

PART IV
Model Paragraph

Tom's Wonderful Morning

Tom woke up at seven o'clock. He felt very rested. After he got dressed he came downstairs. He went into the dining room and saw his favorite breakfast on the table, pancakes and sausage with orange juice and good, hot coffee. After he had breakfast he went outside. It was a beautiful day so he walked to work. Near his office he found a five dollar bill on the sidewalk. What a wonderful way to begin the day!

FREE COMPOSITION

Here is a list of the verbs you learned in this lesson. Use at least five of them in your composition. Verbs: come, stand, find, get, take, see, write, wake, fall, send, build, bend, lend, spend, bring, teach, buy, catch, think, feel, keep, leave, sleep, put, cut, hit, hurt, be, have, go.

My Terrible Morning
or
My Wonderful Morning

LESSON 17A
Combining Sentences IV

In an earlier lesson we learned how to combine two sentences in this manner:

EXAMPLE   John is a student.   Tom is a student.
           John is a student and Tom is too.

Here is a similar way to combine the same two sentences:

           John is a student and so is Tom.

EXERCISE   *In the space provided, make each pair of sentence into one sentence by using this method.*

1. I'm going to watch television tonight.   George is going to watch television tonight.

2. We were tired after the dance.   The musicians were tired after the dance.

3. We are going to have a vacation soon.   The other students are going to have a vacation soon.

4. French and Italian are Romance languages.   Spanish and Portuguese are Romance languages.

We can also use this method in sentences in the simple present.

EXAMPLE   John lives in Plainfield and so <u>does</u> Fred.
           George Brown enjoyed his vacation and so <u>did</u> Alice Allen.

EXERCISE   *In the space provided, make each pair of sentences into one sentence, using the new method.*

1. John ate eggs for breakfast.   I ate eggs for breakfast.

2. Mr. Gillespie plays the trumpet.   Mr. Davis plays the trumpet.

3. I read the assignment.   Roberto read the assignment.

4. Jack went shopping.   Rita went shopping.

We can use this method in sentences with *other auxiliaries*.

EXAMPLE   Ann <u>will be</u> at the party and so <u>will</u> Louise.

EXERCISE   *In the space provided, make each pair of sentences into one sentence, using the new method.*

1. Carlos can speak Spanish.   Manuel can speak Spanish.

2. We'll have a test tomorrow.   They'll have a test tomorrow.

3. I'll be at your party.   Fred will be at your party.

4. My sister can play the piano.   Her friend can play the piano.

EXERCISE   *In the space provided, change each sentence to a sentence with <u>and so.</u>*

1. Marie comes to school on the bus and I do too.

2. Joe went to a party last night and I did too.

3. My brother can play chess and I can too.

4. My room is comfortable and Mary's is too.

5. My wife was born in Cuba and I was too.

6. My roommate likes jazz and I do too.

Here is another way to combine two sentences into one.

EXAMPLE   John is a student.   Tom is a student.
<u>Both John and Tom are students.</u>

Note: **We have made the subject plural, so we must make the verb plural, also.**

EXERCISE   *In the spaces provided, change the sentences in the last exercise into one sentence, using <u>both.</u>*

1.

2.

90

3.

4.

5.

6.

We can combine negative sentences in this manner.

EXAMPLE   Fred wasn't in class yesterday and neither was Joe.

Notice two things: the word is not <u>either</u> but <u>neither,</u> and the second verb is in the *affirmative*. (Neither is a kind of negative form).

EXERCISE   *In the space provided, combine each pair of sentences into one sentence, using <u>neither.</u>*

1. This lesson isn't difficult.   The last one wasn't difficult.

2. I wasn't tired last night.   Tom wasn't tired last night.

3. I'm not going home for Christmas.   My roommate isn't going home for Christmas.

4. I'm not a good swimmer.   My sister isn't a good swimmer.

The same method can be used with other auxiliaries.

EXAMPLE   I didn't come to class yesterday and neither did George.

EXERCISE   *In the space provided, combine each pair of sentences into one sentence, using <u>neither.</u>*

1. My friends can't understand American newspapers.   I can't understand American newspapers.

2. Harry didn't watch television last night.   George didn't watch television last night.

3. My roommate doesn't have much time to go to parties.   I don't have much time to go to parties.

4. Tom doesn't want to go home.   I don't want to go home.

We can also combine negative sentences by making the subject plural, as we did in the method using <u>both</u>.

EXAMPLE   Neither Tom nor I is a teacher.

*Note.*that the word is <u>nor</u>, not <u>or</u>, that the verb is in the *affirmative*, and that it is *singular*.

EXERCISE   *In the space provided, change each of the sentences in the last exercise to one sentence, using <u>nor</u>.*

1.

2.

3.

4.

PART II
Model Paragraph

My wife was born in this country and so was I. She speaks English fluently and so do I. She is a good cook and so am I. She likes to watch television in the evenings and so do I. She stayed up late last night and so did I. Both my wife and I like to stay up late.

EXERCISE   *Copy the paragraph, but change all the sentences to the* **negative.**

My wife wasn't

LESSON 17B
Combining Sentences IV

PART III
And so, Both, Neither-nor

EXERCISE *In the space provided, make each pair of sentences into one sentence, using* <u>and so.</u>

1. Tom came to school on the bus this morning.   I came to school on the bus this morning.

2. My brother has a wonderful wife.   I have a wonderful wife.

3. Mr. Walker's car is out of gas.   Mr. Hooper's car is out of gas.

4. My friend can dance very well.   Her roommate can dance very well.

5. Angela was a teacher before she married.   Mary was a teacher before she married.

EXERCISE *In the space provided, rewrite the sentences in the last exercises, using* <u>both.</u>

1.

2.

3.

4.

5.

Name _____ Date _____   93

EXERCISE *In the space provided, make each pair of sentences into one sentence, using neither.*

1. Phil didn't go to the dance last night.   Nick didn't go to the dance last night.

2. My coffee wasn't hot this morning.   My eggs weren't hot this morning.

3. Fred doesn't want to go shopping.   Martha doesn't want to go shopping.

4. Joe's house isn't far from here.   Bill's house isn't far from here.

5. My friend can't swim.   I can't swim.

EXERCISE *In the space provided, rewrite the sentences in the last example, using neither-nor.*

1.

2.

3.

4.

5.

PART IV
Model Paragraph

My Friend and I

My friend Joe and and I are alike in many ways. He enjoys dancing and so do I. He likes to read and so do I. I like to go to football games and so does Joe, but he doesn't like to play football and neither do I. Last week we went to a football game. I had a wonderful time and so did Joe. Afterward, we went to a restaurant and both he and I had a good dinner. Neither Joe nor I knows how to cook, so he often eats out and so do I. I enjoy being with my friend Joe because he and I enjoy the same things.

My _____ and I

LESSON 18A
Phrases

PART I
Phrases Using Sentences,
Prepositions, and the -ing Verb Form

In Lesson Thirteen we learned how to change a sentence into a *phrase*.

EXAMPLE   My shoes are tight.   <u>my tight shoes</u>

Here is another way to make a sentence into a phrase.

EXAMPLE   The book is on the table.   <u>the book on the table</u>

We do this so we can use the phrase in a new sentence.

EXAMPLE   <u>The book on the table</u> is new.
I bought <u>the book on the table.</u>

You can see that this kind of phrase is different from the phrases in Lesson Thirteen because the words that describe the subject come *after* the subject.

EXERCISE   *In the space provided, change the following sentences into phrases.*

    1. The food is in the cafeteria.

    2. The bank is on the corner.

    3. The class is in Room 13.

    4. The coffee is in my cup.

    5. The words are in Lesson Seventeen.

So, we can see that the sentence <u>The book on the table is new.</u> is really two sentences combined: <u>The book is on the table.</u>   <u>The book is new.</u>

Name _____ *Date* _____   97

In the space provided, make each pair of sentences into one sentence by changing one of the sentences into a phrase.

1. The food is in the cafeteria.   The food is hot.

2. I went to the bank.   The bank is on the corner.

3. I am in the class.   The class is in Room 13.

4. The coffee is in my cup.   The coffee is cold.

5. The words are in Lesson Seventeen.   The words are difficult.

When the sentence shows *possession*, we can make phrases by using the preposition <u>with</u>.

EXERCISE   The man has a car.   <u>the man with the car</u>

Notice the change of article. The car is now *identified* (see Lesson Eight).

EXERCISE   *In the space provided, change these sentences into phrases by using <u>with</u>.*

1. The boy has a pretty sister.

2. The book has nice pictures.

3. The house has a red roof.

4. The shoes have high heels.

5. The teacher has a loud voice.

At other times, we can use the preposition <u>in</u>.

EXAMPLE   The man is wearing a white suit.   <u>the man in the white suit</u>

EXERCISE   *In the space provided, change the following sentences to phrases by using <u>in</u>.*

1. The boy is wearing a red shirt.

2. The girl is wearing a green dress.

3. The man is wearing brown slacks.

In the space provided, make each pair of sentences into one sentence by making one of the sentences into a phrase.

1. The boy has a pretty sister.   The boy is my roommate.

2. I like the book.   The book has pretty pictures.

3. The house has a red roof.   The house is very old.

4. The shoes have high heels.   The shoes are new.

5. I hear the teacher.   The teacher has a loud voice.

6. The boy is wearing a red shirt.   The boy is a student.

7. I know the girl.   The girl is wearing a red dress.

8. The man is wearing brown slacks.   The man is my father.

We can also keep the -ing form of the verb when we make the phrase.

EXAMPLE   The boy is wearing new shoes.   the boy wearing (the) new shoes

EXERCISE   *In the space provided, change the following sentences to phrases, using the -ing form of the verb.*

1. The car is coming down the street.

2. The dog is lying on the rug.

3. The men are working in the street.

EXERCISE   *In the space provided, make each pair of sentences into one sentence by making one of the sentences into a phrase. Keep the -ing form of the verb in the phrase.*

1. The car is coming down the street.   The car is moving too fast.

2. The dog is lying on the rug.   The dog is asleep.

3. The men are working in the street.   The men look tired.

EXERCISE   *Rewrite the following paragraph by combining each pair of
sentences into one sentence.*

I have an apartment. The apartment is on Main Street. The apartment
has pictures. The pictures are on the walls. I have a color television. The
color television is in the living room. I have a refrigerator. The refrigerator
is in the kitchen. I have a little radio. The radio is beside my bed. I like
my little apartment. The apartment is on Main Street.

PART III
Phrases Using Sentences,
Prepositions, and the -ing Verb Form

EXERCISE   *In the space provided, change the following sentences to phrases.*

1. The picture is on the table.

2. The dishes are in the cupboard.

3. The magazines are on the table.

4. The milk is in the refrigerator.

5. The cigars are in the drawer.

EXERCISE   *In the space provided, make each pair of sentences into one sentence.*

1. The picture is on the table.   The picture is pretty.

2. The dishes are in the cupboard.   The dishes are new.

3. I read the magazines.   The magazines are on the table.

4. The milk is in the refrigerator.   The milk is cold.

5. I bought the cigars.   The cigars are in the drawer.

EXERCISE   *In the space provided, make the following sentences into phrases by using* <u>*in.*</u>

1. The girl is wearing a fur coat.

2. The woman is wearing an evening gown.

3. The man is wearing a sports jacket.

EXERCISE   *In the space provided, make the following sentences into phrases using* with.

1. The little girl has a doll.

2. The carpenter has a hammer.

3. The police officer has a big nose.

EXERCISE   *In the space provided, make each pair of sentences into one sentence.*

1. The woman is wearing a fur coat.   The woman is a model.

2. The singer is wearing an evening gown.   The singer is talented.

3. The man is wearing a sports jacket.   The man is having a beer.

4. The little girl has a doll.   The little girl is crying.

5. The carpenter has a hammer.   The carpenter is looking for the nails.

5. The police officer has a big nose.   The police officer is directing traffic.

EXERCISE   *In the space provided, make each sentence into a phrase by using the* -ing *form of the verb.*

1. The people are walking in the park.

2. The children are watching television.

3. The dogs are barking outside the door.

EXERCISE   *In the space provided, make each pair of sentences into one sentence. Keep the* -ing *form of the verb in each sentence.*

1. The people are walking in the park.   The people look cold.

2. The children are watching television.   The children are laughing.

3. The dogs are barking outside the door.   The dogs are hungry.

This is a picture of my family. The man with the moustache is my father. The lady with the gray hair sitting in the armchair is my mother. The young man next to her in the blue suit is my brother Tim. The girl in the yellow sweater and red skirt next to him is his wife Sally, and the little boy in Sally's lap is my nephew Billy. The girl in the photograph on the table is my sister Lucy. She isn't in the picture because she's studying at a college in California.

FREE COMPOSITION

A Picture of My Family

In the last lesson, we learned how to combine two sentences into one by changing one of the sentences into a phrase.

EXAMPLE   The book is on the table.   The book is new.
<u>The book on the table is new.</u>

We can do the same thing by making one of the sentences into a *clause*. Clauses are different from phrases because they have *both* a noun phrase and a verb.

EXAMPLE   <u>the boy with the book</u>   (phrase)
<u>the boy who has a book</u>   (clause)
<u>the book on the table</u>   (phrase)
<u>the book that is on the table</u> (clause)

When both sentences have the same subject, we use <u>who</u> for the subject of a clause when that subject is a person and <u>that</u> when the subject is not a person.

EXERCISE   *In the space provided, make each of the following sentences into a subject and a clause, following the example* <u>The boy has a book.</u>   <u>the boy who has a book</u>

1. The girl has red hair.

2. The house has a green door.

3. The dishes are in the cupboard.

4. The people are on the bus.

5. The cigarettes are in my pocket.

6. The teacher is wearing glasses.

Clauses can also be used as part of the subject or object of a sentence.

EXAMPLE   <u>The girl who is wearing the red dress</u> is a singer.

EXERCISE   *In the space provided, make each pair of sentences into one sentence by making one sentence into a subject containing a clause.*

1. The girl has red hair.   The girl is my sister.

2. The house has a green door.   The house is new.

3. The dishes are in the cupboard.   The dishes are clean.

4. The people are on the bus.   The people are comfortable.

5. The cigarettes are in my pocket.   The cigarettes are Tom's.

6. The teacher is wearing glasses.   The teacher is Mr. Brown.

Sometimes we take the object of a sentence and make it the *subject* of a new sentence. The *subject* and *verb* of that first sentence then become part of a clause.

EXAMPLE   I know a man   <u>the man whom I know</u>
          I read a book   <u>the book that I read</u>

As we see, when the subject is a person, we use <u>whom</u> and not <u>who.</u> When the subject is not a person we use <u>that,</u> as we did before. Notice also how <u>a</u> becomes <u>the</u> as the subject becomes *identified*.

EXERCISE   *In the space provided, take the **object** of each sentence below and make it into a **subject**. Make the rest of the sentence into a clause. Study the examples above.*

1. I ate a sandwich.

2. I wrote a letter.

3. I know a nice girl.

4. I met an American.

5. I saw a movie.

We can now add this new subject to a verb and object to make a new sentence.

EXAMPLE   I know a man.   The man is a lawyer.
          Step 1: I know a man   <u>the man whom I know</u>
          Step 2: <u>The man whom I know is a lawyer.</u>

EXERCISE *In the space provided, combine each pair of sentences into one sentence by making the first sentence into a subject and clause, and adding it to the second sentence.*

1. I ate a sandwich.   The sandwich was delicious.

2. I wrote a letter.   The letter was funny.

3. I know a nice girl.   The nice girl lives near me.

4. I met an American.   The American was friendly.

5. I saw a movie.   The movie was exciting.

We can also substitute that for whom, as we did before.

EXAMPLE   The man whom I know is a lawyer.
The man that I know is a lawyer.

EXERCISE   *In the space provided, copy the sentences in the last exercise, changing whom to that.*

1.

2.

3.

4.

5.

When the complete sentence and the clause have different subjects, we do not need *any* introducing words for the clause at all. So we can write this kind of clause two ways.

EXAMPLE   The book that I bought was expensive.
The book I bought was expensive.

Remember that we can do this only when the clause *and* the main sentence have *different* subjects.

EXERCISE   *In the space provided, copy the sentences in the last exercise and take out that.*

1.

2.

3.

4.

5.

Exercise Paragraph

*Combine each pair of sentences into one sentence by using <u>who</u> or <u>that</u>
and making one of the sentences into a clause.*

I have a friend. The friend lives at home. I enjoy receiving letters.
She writes the letters to me. She sent me a letter. The letter arrived
yesterday. I felt less lonely after I read the letter. She wrote the letter.

LESSON 19B
Clauses

PART III
Who, That, Whom

EXERCISE   *In the space provided, make each of the following sentences into a subject and a clause with who or that.*

1. The child has an ice cream cone.

2. The book has pictures.

3. The fat man is sitting in the corner.

4. The magazines are on the coffee table.

5. The pictures are hanging on the wall.

6. The young girl is wearing a pretty hat.

EXERCISE   *In the space provided, combine each pair of sentences into one sentence by making the first sentence into a subject and clause and using who or that.*

1. The man is driving a Pinto.   The man is Arthur Brown.

2. The dishes are on the table.   The dishes are new.

3. The girl is standing at the window.   The girl is tall.

4. The food is cooking on the stove.   The food smells delicious.

5. The men are sitting in the car.   The men are police officers.

6. The flowers are in the vase.   The flowers are fresh.

Name _____ *Date* _____   **109**

In the space provided, combine each pair of sentences into one sentence by making the first sentence into a subject and clause and using whom *or* that.

1. I drank some coffee.   The coffee was hot.   The coffee _____

2. I met some people.   The people were nice.

3. I smiled at a girl.   The girl spoke to me.

4. John told some jokes.   The jokes weren't very funny.

5. Bill brought a girl to the party.   The girl was very popular.

6. I bought a shirt.   The shirt was red.

EXERCISE *In the space provided, copy the sentences in the last exercise, and take out the* whom *or* that.

1.

2.

3.

4.

5.

6.

A Famous American

Franklin D. Roosevelt was a man who was a member of a famous and wealthy New York family, a man who was governor of New York State, and a man who was assistant secretary of the Navy. But most of all, he was a man whom Americans remember as the person who was their president from 1932 to 1945. They also remember the many new ideas that he brought to America. For example, the Social Security Agency was established during his administration. This is a government bureau that pays money to retired persons who are more than sixty-five years old. Franklin D. Roosevelt is also the first person who was ever elected president four times. When he died in 1945, the nation mourned the man they had chosen as their leader, the man who had guided the nation through the difficult years of World War II.

FREE COMPOSITION

A Famous (person of *your* country)